and why you should give a damn

Praise for
Free Speech and Why You Should Give a Damn

"This engaging and enlightening book is filled with fascinating stories from past and present, with a diverse cast of characters, who all embody the current, urgent importance of robust freedom of speech. It powerfully shows that such freedom is essential for individual liberty, equality, and full participation in our democratic self-government, especially for people who have traditionally been disempowered. Signe Wilkinson's captivating cartoons, as well as Jonathan Zimmerman's witty prose, spark welcome smiles in service of this book's all-too-serious mission: to revitalize our understanding, support, and exercise of our precious speech rights."

> Nadine Strossen, John Marshall Harlan II Professor of Law Emerita, New York Law School; Immediate Past President, American Civil Liberties Union, and author of *HATE: Why We Should Resist It with Free Speech, Not Censorship*

"Have you noticed how in the past few years, a certain set have decided that you should be ousted from polite society for opinions that seem ordinary or at least up for discussion? This book will show you with words and political cartoons what's happened and where to go from here."

> John H. McWhorter, Professor of Linguistics at Columbia University and Contributing Editor at *The Atlantic*

"A lively, informative journey through the history of efforts to restrict speech in the United States. The book crisply illustrates some of the societal tensions that are inevitable where robust speech is involved. Zimmerman has made an exuberant case for the importance of cherishing such expression."

> Carlos E. Cortés, Professor Emeritus of History, University of California, Riverside

"It is imperative these days for young people to have an understanding of the nature and importance of free speech. In Free Speech and Why You Should Give a Damn, *Jonathan Zimmerman offers an accessible, engaging and compelling portrayal of the history of free speech in our nation and why the citizens of a democracy should both embrace and defend it fiercely. This is a work every young person in America should read."*

> Geoffrey R. Stone, Edward H. Levi Distinguished Professor of Law, University of Chicago and co-author of *The Free Speech Century*

Jonathan Zimmerman's book demonstrates how free speech is the backbone of democracy—and how restricting speech can break America. Free Speech and Why You Should Give a Damn *promises to provide both a kickstart and ample information for vitally important classes on civic education and for later conversations at home and elsewhere. And Signe Wilkinson provides wonderfully appealing illustrations."*

> Cynthia and Sanford Levinson, authors of *Fault Lines in the Constitution*

"At a time when many young Americans harbor doubts about the value of free speech, Jonathan Zimmerman's powerful defense of this democratic principle has never been more urgent. The book is at once lucid and learned, elegant and entertaining. Readers from across the political spectrum will benefit from Zimmerman's distillation of how we arrived at this fraught historical moment, and, I hope, will appreciate anew how protecting free speech is essential to our nation's future."

> Justin Driver, Professor of Law, Yale Law School and author of *The Schoolhouse Gate*

"Jonathan Zimmerman reminds us that, more than just a legal doctrine, for the past century the First Amendment has been central to defining the American character. To come in contact with people speaking of free speech and press, as we do in this book, is to hear about fortitude, bravery and self-doubt; to recognize the importance of compromise and of tolerating discord; and to value creativity and change over always trying to preserve the status quo."

Lee C. Bollinger, President of Columbia University and co-author of *The Free Speech Century*

"This pithy, witty and ingenious volume offers an engaging and urgent reminder to young people of why they have a stake in free speech. A look back at historical struggles underscores that free speech has been a catalyst for progress, pushing forward the causes and movements that have rendered a better world. As we fight new battles for social justice, free speech remains an indispensable tool and set of protections for anyone striving to make change."

Suzanne Nossel, Chief Executive Officer, PEN America

""Jonathan Zimmerman's brisk and cheerful trot through free-speech history—enlivened by Signe Wilkinson's zesty drawings—uses humor and passion in equal measure to drive home what's easily forgotten: free speech is the most precious of human rights, the easiest to take for granted—and the easiest to lose. Free Speech and Why You Should Give a Damn *will help us keep it."*

Jonathan Rauch, Senior Fellow, Brookings Institute and author of *Kindly Inquisitors: The New Attacks on Free Thought*

FREE SPEECH
and why you should give a damn

JONATHAN ZIMMERMAN

Cartoons by
SIGNE WILKINSON

A City of Light imprint

New Idea Press
A City of Light Imprint

City of Light Publishing
266 Elmwood Ave., Suite 407
Buffalo, New York 14222

info@CityofLightPublishing.com
www.CityofLightPublishing.com

Book design by Ana Cristina Ochoa

ISBN: 978-1-952536-10-6 (cloth)
ISBN: 978-1-952536-11-3 (ebook)

Printed in Canada
10 9 8 7 6 5 4 3 2 1

Library of Congress Cataloging-in-Publication Data
Names: Zimmerman, Jonathan, 1961- author. | Wilkinson, Signe, 1950-illustrator.
Title: Free speech : and why you should give a damn / Jonathan Zimmerman ; with illustrations by Pulitzer Prize-winning cartoonist, Signe Wilkinson.
Description: Buffalo, New York : New Idea Press, a City of Light imprint, [2021] | Includes bibliographical references. | Summary: "In America we like to think we live in a land of liberty, where everyone can say whatever they want. Throughout our history, however, we have also been quick to censor people who offend or frighten us. We talk a good game about freedom of speech, then we turn around and deny it to others. In this brief but bracing book, historian Jonathan Zimmerman and Pulitzer Prize-winning political cartoonist Signe Wilkinson tell the story of free speech in America: who established it, who has denounced it, and who has risen to its defense. They also make the case for why we should care about it today, when free speech is once again under attack. Across the political spectrum, Americans have demanded the suppression of ideas and images that allegedly threaten our nation. But the biggest danger to America comes not from speech but from censorship, which prevents us from freely governing ourselves. Free speech allows us to criticize our leaders. It lets us consume the art, film, and literature we prefer. And, perhaps most importantly, it allows minorities to challenge the oppression they suffer. Free speech has too often been cast as the enemy of social justice, but that view is belied by our history. Disadvantaged Americans have consistently used free speech to defy the powerful. The only way to make a more just and equitable America is to allow every American to have their say"-- Provided by publisher.
Identifiers: LCCN 2020042668 (print) | LCCN 2020042669 (ebook) | ISBN 9781952536106 (hardcover) | ISBN 9781952536113 (epub) | ISBN 9781952536113 (kindle edition) | ISBN 9781952536113 (mobi) | ISBN 9781952536113 (pdf)
Subjects: LCSH: Freedom of speech--United States. | Censorship--United States--History. | United States. Constitution. 1st Amendment.
Classification: LCC KF4772 .Z458 2021 (print) | LCC KF4772 (ebook) | DDC 323.44/30973--dc23
LC record available at https://lccn.loc.gov/2020042668
LC ebook record available at https://lccn.loc.gov/2020042669

CONTENTS

Why I Wrote This Book

In 1919, the United States government began a massive campaign of violence and espionage against socialists, anarchists, and other dissidents. It was led by Attorney General A. Mitchell Palmer, who warned that "radicals" were spreading "a disease of evil thinking." The only way to protect the nation, Palmer insisted, was to stamp them out. Federal agents compiled a card system listing 200,000 suspects; they also conducted dragnet-style "Palmer Raids" (as mass arrests became known) in pool halls, cafes, and other places where their targets were known to congregate. Roughly 10,000 people were arrested, 3,000 were imprisoned, and more than 500—including the famous labor activist Emma Goldman—were deported.

"Ever since I have been in this country—and I have lived here practically all my life—it has been dinned into my ears that under the institutions of this Democracy one is entirely free to think as he pleases," Goldman said at her deportation hearing. "What becomes of this sacred guarantee of freedom and thought and conscience when persons are being persecuted and driven out for the very motives and purposes for which the pioneers who built up this country laid down their lives?"

To federal judge Learned Hand, likewise, it seemed like the American spirit of liberty had gone into hibernation. "The merry sport of Red-baiting goes on," Hand wrote to Supreme Court Justice Oliver Wendell Holmes. "I really can't get up much sympathy for the victims, but I own a sense of dismay at the increase in all the symptoms of apparent panic." Indeed, Hand argued, the biggest victim of the Palmer Raids was free speech itself. "How far people are getting afraid to speak… I don't know, but I am sure that the public generally is becoming rapidly demoralized in all its sense of proportion and toleration," Hand warned. "For men who are not cock-sure about everything and especially for those who are not damned cock-sure about anything, the skies have a rather sinister appearance."

Almost exactly a century later, the skies are darkening again for free speech in America. To be clear, nobody has been rounded up in Palmer-style raids. But the United States elected a president in 2016 who threatened free speech at every turn. Donald J. Trump called major media outlets "enemies of the people," threatening to revoke their broadcast licenses. He encouraged supporters at his rallies to assault protesters, promising to pay any legal bills that resulted. And he congratulated a Republican congressman for body-slamming a reporter from CNN, one of Trump's staunchest critics. Ironically, Trump held a "social media summit" in 2019 to complain that his own defenders—especially those on the so-called "alt-right"—have been deprived of free speech. Yet his comments at the event confirmed that this president believed speech rights should be reserved for only one category of people: those who support Donald J. Trump. "See, I don't think that the mainstream media is free speech, either, because it's so crooked. It's so dishonest," Trump told the summit. "So to me, free speech is not when you see something good and then you purposely write bad. To me, that's very dangerous speech, and you become angry at it. But that's not free speech." Free speech, in short, is speech that Donald Trump likes. Everything else isn't—or shouldn't be—free at all.

At the same time, though, Trump's critics on the Left eroded free speech in other ways. On college campuses, protesters have interrupted or shouted down pro-Trump speakers. Universities established codes to regulate offensive speech, even after courts found that these policies violated the First Amendment of the United States Constitution. Most alarmingly, growing numbers of young people expressed skepticism about the value of free speech itself. Whereas a third of Americans in 2013 said that the First Amendment "goes too far" in protecting speech, nearly half of people 18-32 agreed with that view. And 60 percent of Americans in their 20s said that "Muslim clergymen who preach hatred against the United States" should not be allowed to do that in their communities, as compared to 43 percent of people in their 40s. At colleges, meanwhile, 71 percent of freshmen in 2015-16 agreed that their institutions should "prohibit racist/ sexist speech on campus," up from 59 percent in 1992. And in 2017, 30 percent of undergraduates—that is, almost one out of three—said that physical violence can be justified to prevent someone from using hateful words.

That bears a sad parallel to Donald Trump, who has endorsed violence against speakers who supposedly injured him with their words. I get it: words hurt. But once "hurt" becomes the way we limit speech, almost nobody will get to speak at all. I realized that when I hosted Mary Beth Tinker in my classroom at the University of Pennsylvania, where Tinker displayed the armband she had worn to her junior high school in 1965 to protest the Vietnam War. The school sent her home, triggering a lawsuit and—eventually—the landmark 1969 Supreme Court decision, *Tinker v. Des*

Moines, which established that students and teachers have the right to free expression. My students told Tinker that she had been fighting the good fight, against an unjust war, so of course she should have been allowed to express herself in school. But racists and sexists and homophobes hurt people, they said, so their speech should not be protected. Instead, it was the duty of the school—and of all of us—to protect vulnerable minorities against hurtful speech. Speech was a tool of the powerful, and we needed to regulate it so everyone else remained safe and sound.

Mary Beth Tinker wasn't having it. At her school in Des Moines, Tinker noted, there were students who had fathers and brothers who were fighting—and dying—in Vietnam.

And here was this snot-nosed kid, wearing a symbol that suggested their loved ones were risking everything for a lie. Did that hurt them? Of course it did. So if you're going to prohibit speech that hurts people, you'll have to censor Mary Beth Tinker's protest as well.

Nor did Tinker accept the trendy claim that free speech is just a weapon of people in power. In 1965, she reminded the audience, she was a 13-year-old girl. Speech was the only power that she had! And once you take it away, it will be that people at the bottom—the people without other kinds of power—that suffer the most. That's why all the great warriors for social justice in American history—including Frederick Douglass, Susan B. Anthony, and Martin Luther King, Jr.— were also zealous advocates of free speech. Only in our own era have these two ideals, social justice and free speech, been pitted against each other.

That's also why this book takes an historical approach. Looking backwards, I hope to remind our readers— particularly the younger ones—how speech has been restricted and censored in the past, especially for Americans who were racial or political minorities. I hope to show how many people sacrificed their lives and livelihoods, just so we could say (and read, and write, and watch) what we want today. And, most of all, I hope to convince you that we must hold fast to these hard-won gains. In the time of Donald J. Trump, when so much hate reverberates through our public sphere, it is tempting to limit free speech to the "good" kind. But that's what Trump threatened to do, of course. Restricting hate speech isn't a form of "resistance" to Trump, as his opponents sometimes claim. It's a capitulation to him, and to the same censorious impulses that have periodically marred America since its founding. We were born in liberty, as Emma Goldman noted, but our belief in it has waned at different times in our history. This is one of those times. This book aims to revive that democratic faith, where everyone—yes, everyone—can have their say.

Pictures have been censored alongside speech, of course, which is one reason why I decided to include Signe Wilkinson's extraordinary political cartoons here. Another is that they can convey ideas in ways that words can't. A cartoon is a particular kind of picture, combining graphics and words to capture our attention and imagination.

Not surprisingly, cartoons have been censored across our history. And cartoonists have fired back, zealously defending the principles and practices of free speech. In a much-reproduced 1915 image from the radical magazine *The Masses*, cartoonist Robert Minor ridiculed Anthony Comstock—the era's leading censor of "immoral" sexual content—by depicting Comstock before a judge, dragging a disheveled young woman by the scruff of her neck. "Your Honor, this woman gave birth to a naked child!" Comstock exclaims.

Since then, cartoonists have skewered every government effort to censor speech, from the Palmer Raids of 1919-20 right up to recent laws against flag desecration. And they have also called upon all of us to open our eyes—and our minds—to different viewpoints, which is the raison d'etre of free speech itself. In a 2017 cartoon, Angelo Lopez depicted a bound and gagged Uncle Sam surrounded by protesters. "My opinions only!" they shout. "Free speech for those I agree with!"

In 1988, fortunately, the Supreme Court declared that cartoons themselves were a form of protected speech under the First Amendment. The case involved a *Hustler* magazine parody advertisement, lampooning Moral Majority founder Jerry Falwell as an incestuous drunk. In his decision, Justice William Rehnquist noted that cartoonists had satirized every leading public figure—including Lincoln and both Roosevelt presidents—and that "our political discourse would have been considerably poorer without them."

He was right. But we can't rely on judges to protect free speech, which will survive only if the American people believe in it. That was the key insight of Learned Hand, who wrote what may be our country's best- known tribute to free speech in *The Spirit of Liberty* in 1944, two decades after the Palmer Raids:

> I often wonder whether we do not rest our hopes too much upon constitutions, upon laws, upon courts. Liberty lies in the hearts of men and women; when it dies there no constitution, no law, no court can save it.

In the end, free speech depends on our faith in each other. We have come too far to turn back from it now.

CHAPTER ONE

Free Speech Allows Us to Criticize Our Leaders

A few years ago, a student from the People's Republic of China came to see me in my office. She was struggling in my class, which required students to participate in group discussions. In the United States, she told me, people were expected to share their opinions, especially on political matters. But in China, it was the opposite. "We don't talk about the government, especially if there's something we don't like," she whispered. "It's too dangerous."

She was right, and not just about China. Nearly half the world's people live in countries where freedom of speech is at "extreme risk," according to a 2019 research report. Hundreds of journalists have been jailed or murdered; most notoriously,

Washington Post contributor Jamal Khashoggi—a frequent critic of Saudi Arabia's rulers—was killed and dismembered by a team of Saudi assassins in 2018. Twenty-five governments imposed internet blackouts that year, preventing critics from circulating information and opinions. Police in Hong Kong

arrested 400 pro-democracy demonstrators on New Year's Day 2020, bringing the total to about 7,000 arrests since protests started there six months earlier. Around the world, thousands of other citizen-activists were harassed, imprisoned, or killed simply for saying or writing what they thought.

That used to happen in America, too, especially when the nation was at war. For most of our history, indeed, dissent during wartime was illegal or highly restricted. From the skirmishes with France in the late 1790s to the early stages of the Vietnam conflict in the 1960s, Americans were fined, imprisoned, or deported for criticizing their government. Only in the last half-century have we been able to protest wartime activity without fear of state reprisal or repression. Like the poor, war will always be with us. But we are free to denounce it—and the people who wage it—in ways that would have shocked prior generations of dissidents. They put their lives on the line, so that we could be free.

So if you have ever written an angry letter to the editor about a government policy, thank the brave souls who came before us. Thank them, too, if you have posted on the Internet to oppose the president or any other politician. And thank them if you have attended a political protest, against war or anything else. I publish dozens of newspaper columns every year, and most of them criticize our elected leaders. Nobody from the government has threatened me any way; no one has come in the night for me or my family. I'm grateful to live in a country that lets us lambaste our leaders in whatever way we choose.

But I also know how hard it was to win this freedom, and how easy it would be to lose it. That's why we always have to be on the alert about defending the right to criticize our government, especially when America is at war. According to the much-quoted maxim attributed to Thomas Jefferson, eternal vigilance is the price of freedom. It turns out that Jefferson probably didn't write that, but it doesn't matter. Whoever coined the phrase got it exactly right.

In 1798, when America was barely two decades old, a wide swath of Americans feared it was coming to an end. The threat originated in France, which had attacked vessels flying the American flag and had also demanded bribes (via three anonymous emissaries, identified only as X, Y, and Z) to negotiate an end to the hostilities. But the biggest peril, critics alleged, came from the Americans who were doing France's bidding at home.

Led by President John Adams, the ruling Federalist Party used the so-called "XYZ Affair" to push through the Alien and Sedition Acts. The acts nearly tripled the span that immigrants would need to reside in the United States before gaining citizenship, from five to fourteen years; they authorized Adams to expel "dangerous" (read: pro-France) aliens; and, most notoriously, the new measures established fines and jail sentences for anyone who "shall write, print, utter or publish… false, scandalous, and malicious writing or writings against the government of the United States." In short, dissent became illegal.

And it made a certain kind of sense, as censorship always does. At a moment of international violence and gamesmanship, why should we let Americans play for the other team? The safest move was to shut them down, at least until the danger had passed. Dissidents would invoke their sacred rights of liberty, of course, but that was just a ruse to destroy the country and the shared values it needed to survive. "Liberty of the press and of opinion is calculated to destroy all confidence between man and man," one Federalist member of Congress declared. "It leads to a dissolution of every bond of union."

The most famous person to be prosecuted under the Alien and Sedition Acts was Vermont Rep. Matthew Lyon, who became the first member of Congress to be convicted of a crime; several months later, he was re-elected while in prison. After Jefferson defeated Adams in 1800, the acts expired. But the template had been set: whenever the nation found itself under threat, whether real or imagined, it would take measures to muzzle free speech.

It happened again during the Civil War, which was a truly existential crisis for the United States. After eleven Southern states seceded from the Union, Abraham Lincoln declared that "all Rebels and Insurgents" in the Confederacy—and, pointedly, "their aiders and abettors within the United States"—would be subject to trial and punishment by military courts. Between 13,000 and 38,000 civilians were arrested over the course of the war, mostly for draft evasion.

But free speech suffered, too. One Illinois citizen was arrested for saying that "anyone who enlists is a God Damned fool;" an Ohioan, for proclaiming that "not 50 soldiers will fight to free Negroes;" and a man in New Jersey, for saying that whites who fought on the Union side were "no better than a goddamned nigger." The most prominent person arrested was former Ohio Rep. Clement Vallandigham, a leading "Copperhead" (as anti-war Northerners were called), who gave a departing speech on the floor of Congress denouncing Lincoln for waging a "war for the Negro."

Several months later, Vallandigham told a large crowd that "King Lincoln" had trampled on the liberties of whites. Military authorities threw him in jail and closed the *Chicago Times*, which had criticized both the war and his arrest; all told, 300 antiwar newspapers in the North were suppressed. To Lincoln, censorship was a simple military necessity. "Armies cannot be maintained unless desertions shall be punished by the severe penalty of death," he wrote. "Must I shoot a simple-minded solider boy who deserts, while I must not touch a hair of a wily agitator who induces him to desert?"

Leave aside that Lincoln—as a young Congressman—had criticized President James Polk for his conduct of the Mexican War, as several Copperhead newspapers noted. The real problem with censorship was that it took the justice of the war as a given, instead of allowing citizens to deliberate it. "The question of prosecuting the war, or concluding a peace, can not be intelligently decided till we hear from both sides, and all sides," Vallandigham's lawyer argued, in an unsuccessful attempt to win his release from prison.

Especially given the racist stench of his rhetoric, it is certainly tempting to conclude that the government had every right to lock up Vallandigham. But white supporters of the war were hardly exempt from racism; indeed, Lincoln himself gave several speeches blatantly asserting the superiority of whites over Blacks. Most of all, censoring antiwar citizens made a mockery of the much-vaunted "battle cry of freedom" at the heart of the Union cause.

Lincoln slowly came to the same conclusion, revoking the order to close the *Chicago Times* and scolding his own generals for shuttering other newspapers. Censorship was anti-democratic, denying the people the right to make up their own minds. And once that practice became established, it could just as easily be turned against its advocates. "Did it ever occur to you that the next election may put an entirely different face upon affairs?" warned Connecticut Senator Lyman Trumbull, a strong Unionist who nevertheless opposed censoring antiwar opinions. If the other side came to power, Trumbull worried, it would muzzle people like him.

Unfortunately, this was a lesson that Americans have kept forgetting. Over the next century, whenever the United States went to war, dissidents would pay the price. As soon as the country entered World War I in 1917, Woodrow Wilson—who had been re-elected the previous year on the platform, "He kept us out of the war"—signed several draconian laws that all but eliminated legal criticism of it.

The Espionage Act of 1917 barred the publication of information that "might be useful to the enemy" or "cause disaffection in the military." It also gave the Postmaster General authority to exclude "treasonable or anarchic" material from the U.S mails. The following year, the Sedition Act prohibited "disloyal, profane, scurrilous, or abusive language" about the U.S. Constitution, government, or flag. That meant that any kind of critique of the country—not just dissent against the war—was now against the law.

Conformity was enforced by a dense network of federal agents and voluntary organizations, which coordinated with the government to spy upon potential dissidents. Or it was simply outsourced to mobs, who terrorized their fellow citizens while the authorities looked the other way. In Oklahoma, a former minister who opposed the sale of bonds to finance the war was tarred and feathered; in California, a brewery worker who made pro-German remarks suffered the same fate.

Meanwhile, across the country pacifists and other critics of the war were being thrown in jail. Filmmaker Robert Goldstein was imprisoned for producing a movie about the American Revolution, *The Spirit of '76*, which included a scene showing British soldiers massacring women and children. In prior years, a judge ruled, that scene would have been allowed, but Britain was an ally now, so any criticism of it might harm the war effort. "Between Wilson and his brigades of informers, spies, volunteer detectives, perjurers and complaisant judges … the liberty of the citizen has pretty well vanished in America," complained journalist H. L. Mencken.

The "complaisant judges" initially included Supreme Court Justice Oliver Wendell Holmes, who upheld the Espionage Act in his famous (or, to civil libertarians, infamous) *Schenck v. United States* decision of 1919. The general secretary of the Socialist Party of Philadelphia, Charles Schenck, had been arrested and convicted for printing and circulating 15,000 flyers urging men to resist conscription. Given the wartime context, Holmes argued, Schenck's speech was tantamount to falsely shouting fire in a crowded theatre; it presented a "clear and present danger" to security, he argued, so the government was within its rights to suppress it.

Holmes would later come to regret his opinion in this case, which could be used to censor pretty much anything. Just a few months later, in *Abrams v. United States*, the Court upheld the conviction of defendants who had distributed leaflets condemning the American invasion of Russia and other efforts to impede the Bolshevik Revolution. This time Holmes was in the minority, issuing a stinging dissent that eventually became a sacred text in the struggle for free speech. The leaflets in question were written in Yiddish, Holmes noted, and—unlike the Schenck flyers—they posed no immediate danger to the war effort. Instead, Holmes argued, the real danger lay in the effort to squelch them. "Persecution for the expression of opinions seems to me perfectly logical," Holmes acknowledged. "If you have no doubt of your premises or your power and want a certain result with all your heart you naturally express your wishes in law and sweep away all opposition."

But that assumed that the censor had a monopoly on truth, which was the most destructive fantasy of all. The best information and opinion was more likely to emerge from a "free trade in ideas," Holmes concluded, which would never work if citizens were restricted in the expression of those same ideas.

Holmes is justly venerated for this opinion, so it's easy to forget that free speech remained a minority opinion—on the Supreme Court, and within the wider American public—for the next fifty years. In the Smith Act of 1940, Congress prohibited citizens from advocating or abetting the overthrow of the government by force or violence. The obvious target was the Communist Party, which had made a small foothold in the United States during the Great Depression. But when the United States entered World War Two in December 1941, its enemies were fascist rather than Communist. Indeed, "Uncle Joe" Stalin and the Soviet Union became our allies against Hitler, Mussolini, and Tojo.

So the government hounded right-wing extremists like William Dudley Pelley, who proudly dubbed himself "The American Hitler" and lambasted the "Jew Deal" of president Franklin D. "Rosenfeld." The Roosevelt administration's campaign to censor Pelley and other home-grown anti-Semites was egged on by left-leaning voices like the *Nation* magazine, which called on the government to "curb the fascist press." But when the war ended, and Communism re-emerged as the biggest security threat, the *Nation* would itself be banned from school districts and libraries around the country because of its allegedly "Red" slant.

Most notoriously, thousands of teachers, civil servants, and other citizens were jailed, harassed, or hounded out of their jobs for prior or present-day affiliations with Communist or so-called "fellow-traveler" organizations. In Texas, joining the Communist Party was punishable by 20 years in jail; in Michigan, the penalty was life in prison.

The justification for these restrictions was the same that previous censors had invoked: there's a war going on, and we need to win it. It was a Cold War, of course, pitting the United States against the Soviet Union in an epic battle for the hearts and minds of the globe. But that was all the more reason to police speech, lest anyone on our side consider joining the other one. As in World War One, an interlocking nexus of government agents and private organizations monitored political expression to make sure it followed the (American) party line. The result was a spirit of fear and conformity, sharply limiting the spectrum of acceptable public opinion.

"The great danger of this period is not inflation, not the national debt, not atomic warfare," wrote Supreme Court Justice William Douglas, in a 1952 article for The New York Times. "The great, the critical danger, is that we will so limit or narrow the range of permissible discussion and permissible thought that we will become victims of the orthodox school."

Five years later, in 1957, Douglas would join five other justices in throwing out the Smith Act convictions of several Communist Party officials. Although the Communist Party supported the overthrow of the government as an "abstract doctrine," the court wrote, the members in question did not advocate specific action to that end. So the case failed Holmes's clear-and-present danger test, penalizing citizens not for their threat to safety and order but for their point of view.

"Governmental suppression of causes and beliefs seems to me to be the very antithesis of what our Constitution stands for," wrote Justice Hugo Black, in a concurring opinion. "The First Amendment provides the only kind of security system that can preserve a free government—one that leaves the way wide open for people to favor, discuss, advocate, or incite causes and doctrines however obnoxious and antagonistic such views may be to the rest of us."

Over the next decade, the country would finally become open for antiwar protest as well. Demonstrations against our overseas wars have become so ubiquitous that it's easy to forget how long they were suppressed, and how recently they were allowed.

The Vietnam War was the first moment when antiwar protest became legal and protected, if not uniformly welcomed and accepted. In rapid succession, the Supreme Court overturned the arrests of people who mocked the armed forces by donning military uniforms in a theater production, of a man who sewed a U.S. flag on the seat of his pants to protest the war, and of another who wore a jacket into a courthouse bearing the words "Fuck the Draft." As these examples illustrate, the will to censor was alive and well in the United States. But the courts were no longer willing to tolerate the state suppression of "unpatriotic" sentiment, despite a long and ugly pattern of the same.

JONATHAN ZIMMERMAN

In 1989, the Supreme Court would nullify laws in 48 states that barred desecration of the American flag, earning a censure from the United States Senate—which voted 97-3 to condemn the decision—and also from president George H. W. Bush. "Flag burning is wrong, dead wrong," Bush pronounced. But it was also a protected right, for the first time in our history. "The Government may not prohibit the expression of an idea simply because society finds the idea itself offensive or disagreeable," Justice William Brennan ruled.

That's easy to endorse when the offending idea is something like flag-burning, which has lost much of its shock value in recent years. It's a lot harder to support protections for racist and anti-Semitic speech, which is still very much with us. But the courts defended that as well, insisting that bigots have the same speech rights as anybody else.

In 1964, Ku Klux Klan leader Clarence Brandenburg was filmed at a KKK rally warning that "there might have to be some revengeance [sic] taken" against the federal government for suppressing "the white, Caucasian race." He was arrested and sentenced under an Ohio law barring speech that advocated illegal acts. The Supreme Court overturned his conviction, on the same ground that it voided bans on anti-government threats by Communists: absent evidence of "imminent lawless action," the court ruled, even the most blatantly hateful speech was protected under the Constitution.

the FLAG... the FREEDOM for WHICH IT STANDS

Since then, every federal court that has examined hate speech has come to the same conclusion. In 1992, the Supreme Court struck down a St. Paul, Minnesota ordinance prohibiting speech that was likely to arouse "anger, alarm or resentment in others on the basis of race, color, creed, religion, or gender." Ultimately, the court ruled, public officials would be called upon to decide what was truly hateful and what was not. And that's not a call that any of us should want our government to make.

If you think otherwise, perhaps you place too much trust in the government. After the World Trade Center and Pentagon attacks of September 11, 2001, the Patriot Act gave law enforcement officials new powers to infiltrate political and religious groups, to covertly review emails, and to eavesdrop on attorney-client communications. Several of its provisions were struck down by the courts following objections from civil libertarians, whom attorney general John Ashcroft accused of giving "ammunition to our enemies." But he was wrong, just like every other persecutor in our long and inglorious history of censorship. Some of the Islamic extremists targeted by the government had truly noxious views, denouncing America for harboring gays and other "infidels." So long as they were not actively plotting to harm their fellow citizens, however, they had the same right to spout their bigoted drivel as Clement Vallandigham and William Dudley Pelley before them.

The price of freedom is not simply eternal vigilance against state overreach, as Jefferson supposedly said (but probably didn't). It's also allowing people whom you despise to have their say, no matter how much it hurts. "If there is any principle in the Constitution that more imperatively calls for attachment than any other, it is the principle of free thought—not free thought for those who agree with us, but freedom for the thought we hate," Oliver Wendell Holmes wrote in 1929.

Holmes' plea came in yet another one of his dissenting opinions, this time on behalf of a pacifist who had refused to swear an oath to "take up arms in defense of her country." And surely, pacifists were as hated by their fellow citizens as any white racist or Islamic extremist today.

This is precisely why we need to be vigilant in defending free speech, which simply cannot exist if the government picks and chooses what is acceptable speech and what is not. In a country marred by prejudice and inequality of many stripes, censorship will inevitably harm the people with the least power. Its most common victims have been racial and sexual minorities rather than racists and sexists. Once you empower the censors, as Lyman Trumbull warned, you don't know whom they will target. And sooner or later, they will come after you.

CHAPTER TWO

Free Speech Allows Racial Minorities, Women, LGBTQ, and Working-class Americans to Challenge Their Oppression

I'm a liberal Democrat. I'm pro-choice, pro-Obamacare, and vehemently anti-Trump.

But I'm also a strong supporter of free speech, which marks me as "conservative" in many left-leaning circles today. Here's how the argument usually proceeds.

White people—especially white men—dominate the country. And one way they do so is by promoting free speech, which is a tool of repression masked as a route to liberation. White guys (like myself) set the rules of engagement, defending hate speech and shouting "censorship" whenever they don't get their way. Meanwhile, racial minorities and women—the most frequent targets of that hate speech—suffer verbal attacks on their very right to exist.

In this context, "free" speech is anything but free. Its costs are borne by the most disadvantaged among us, who must absorb daily slurs, slights, and barbs. No wonder folks on top are so hot on free speech! It preserves their interests, even as it harms those at the bottom.

Tell that to Frederick Douglass. Or Susan B. Anthony. Or Eugene V. Debs. Or Martin Luther King, Jr. Every great champion of the poor and dispossessed in United States history has also been a champion of free speech, which allowed them to critique inequality and oppression. That's why Douglass called free speech "the great moral renovator of society and government." Without it, people who were oppressed and subjugated could not call public attention to their plight. Lacking other resources and privileges, free speech was their only weapon. If you took that away, they had nothing.

That's also why the people in control often tried to suppress or limit speech—they understood its power, just as Frederick Douglass did. If enslaved people or women or industrial laborers were allowed to speak their minds, they might succeed in changing the minds of others. And then what? In time, the whole edifice of advantage and privilege would come crumbling down.

So free speech was dangerous, but for the opposite reason that contemporary critics invoke: it threatened established hierarchies, rather than reinforcing them. Only our present-day myopia makes free speech look conservative or even reactionary. It was—and remains—a radical idea, representing the only real path for emancipating ourselves.

The first mass censorship campaign in the United States began after Nat Turner's slave rebellion in 1831, which killed roughly 60 white men, women, and children. Pointing to the literacy skills of Turner, who could read the Bible and saw himself as a prophet, Southern states passed measures that made it illegal to teach slaves and free Blacks how to read and write. They also prohibited the publication of anti-slavery opinions; in Virginia, state legislators even barred the reprinting of anti-slavery comments that were made during their own debate on the topic.

Meanwhile, Southerners tried to block anti-slavery literature from the U.S. mails. Mobs broke into post offices, seized anti-slavery pamphlets, and burned them on the streets. There were also efforts to censor and suppress anti-slavery activity in the North, where crowds routinely raided abolitionist meetings and assaulted participants.

So debate on the subject was severely limited, which is just what slavery defenders and apologists wanted. "Democracy... must examine, compare, and analyze, and how can it do this without freedom of inquiry and discussion?" one Boston newspaper asked, condemning the mob violence. "To argue that there are subjects, which ought not to be discussed... is in reality to argue that the people are not capable of self-government."

This is another premise of censors, in all times and places: we can't let the public speak or listen, because it might come to the wrong conclusion. North Carolina banned an 1857 book by a white Tar Heel author, Hilton Helper, who argued that slavery had harmed the Southern economy and impoverished non-slaveholding whites. That was a dagger at the heart of the South, lawmakers said, so censoring the book was a simple matter of self-defense.

Two years later, when abolitionist John Brown attacked Harper's Ferry, critics pointed to Helper's book—without any evidence—as the inspiration for the raid. A minister who had distributed the book was sentenced to jail and a whipping under a North Carolina statute barring literature that caused slaves to "become discontented." When he slipped out of the state, the legislature amended the law to make circulating such material punishable by death.

The censorship campaign extended into the halls of Congress, where Southern lawmakers and their Northern allies pushed through "gag rules" barring anti-slavery petitions from the floor. If they could stifle speech about slavery, legislators reasoned, they might also squelch efforts to restrict or eliminate it.

The effect was the opposite, however, marking another frequent characteristic of censorship: it tends to produce precisely the activity that it seeks to inhibit. The gag rule made a hero of John Quincy Adams, a former president and the leading anti-slavery voice in Congress. It also allowed anti-slavery advocates to identify their cause with freedom of thought and expression, which lay at the heart of the American experiment itself.

This is why Frederick Douglass chose Boston for his most famous paean to free speech, which he delivered in the city's Music Hall after a mob had broken up an anti-slavery meeting in the same venue. Boston was the fount of the American Revolution, which enshrined human liberty as its pre-eminent value; if Americans turned their backs on this tradition, Douglass warned, they would also close themselves off to collective growth and progress. "To suppress free speech is a double wrong. It violates the rights of the hearer as well as those of the speaker," Douglass declared. "It is just as criminal to rob a man of his right to speak and hear as it would be to rob him of his money."

Meanwhile, elsewhere in Massachusetts, the gag rule prompted grateful constituents of anti-slavery Congressman Chauncey Knapp to present him with a gift he could take to Washington: a revolver. It was inscribed with the words "Free Speech," which had become indispensable in the fight against slavery.

After the Civil War, workers in the growing movement for labor unions recognized free speech as central to their cause. Their bosses knew that too, which is why they sought to muzzle pro-union sentiment whenever they could. In the nationwide Pullman Strike of 1894, led by socialist leader Eugene Debs, railway owners prevailed upon federal authorities to issue an injunction barring union leaders from urging workers to strike; arrested for violating the injunction, Debs was sentenced to six months in prison.

Federal courts also issued prohibitions on boycotts, barring union newspapers from instructing readers not to patronize certain companies. Such restrictions were "an invasion of the liberty of the Press and the Right to free speech," union leader Samuel Gompers declared in 1907, adding that the principles at stake extended beyond the matter at hand. "Tomorrow it may be another publication," he noted, "and the present injunction may then be quoted as sacred precedent for further encroachments upon the liberties of the people."

He was right. In 1919, when Seattle labor leaders called a general strike, the city prohibited "language tending … to arouse the anger and incite the antagonism or wrath of the citizens," which could be used to bar almost any speech that authorities wished to remove. There were also injunctions issued against picketing, which became so rare that many members of the public did not know there was a strike on at all.

Three years later, during another national railroad strike, federal authorities barred any effort to promote the strike via telegram, telephone, or word of mouth. Journalist William Allen White placed a pro-union sign in the window of his Kansas newspaper, the *Emporia Gazette*, daring the state governor to arrest him. Charges against White were eventually dropped, but the editor of a pro-labor newspaper in Memphis received six months in jail for calling strikebreakers "snakes" and "dirty scabs."

Muckraking journalist Upton Sinclair was arrested in 1923 for holding a pro-union meeting on Liberty Hill, high above the Los Angeles harbor, where observers noted the irony of the protest site's name. To reinforce it, Sinclair recited a few words of the First Amendment before police ushered him away.

A year later, striking silk workers in Paterson, New Jersey also read aloud passages of the Constitution. When a policeman asked to see his permit for the demonstration, one unionist held up the Bill of Rights and announced, "This is my permit." Roger Baldwin, founder of the newly formed American Civil Liberties Union, visited the town's chief of police the next day. "Chief, you talk as if you were the censor of who could talk in this town, what they can say and where they can say it," Baldwin said. "Well I am," the chief replied. By the end of the 1920s, Baldwin estimated, nine of ten battles taken on by the ACLU concerned the free-speech rights of American workers.

Another common target of censorship during these years was the women's suffrage movement, which won the Nineteenth Amendment—guaranteeing voting rights for both sexes—in 1920. But right up to the final victory, authorities tried to stall the movement by denying speech rights to its members. Police officials routinely refused to issue permits for parades and protests by suffrage marchers, which was the simplest way to shut them down. Or authorities looked the other way while hecklers threw corks, apple cores, and lit cigars at female demonstrators.

At a 1917 "silent picket" in front of the White House, shortly after the United States entered World War I, suffragists carried banners comparing Woodrow Wilson to the German Kaiser. Mobs engulfed them, spitting at the protesters and grabbing their "traitorous" banners. Officials arrested leading suffragists like Alice Paul, who was served worm-infested food in prison; staging a hunger strike, she was force-fed liquids by her jailers.

After more than 500 suffrage protesters had been arrested, Wilson relented and agreed to support the Nineteenth Amendment. In a message to Congress, he called it "vital to winning the war." Indeed, the popular tide had turned in favor of women's suffrage. As was often the case, censoring people made them more sympathetic in the public eye.

That was also true for the nascent birth control movement, which ultimately benefited from government efforts to suppress it. Its most prominent leader was the feminist nurse and journalist Margaret Sanger, who in 1914 started her own magazine, *The Woman Rebel*. "What rebel women claim is the right to be lazy," Sanger announced, in its inaugural issue. "The right to be an un-married mother. The right to destroy. The right to create. The right to live. The right to love." The magazine also published information about contraception, which got Sanger indicted on four counts of obscenity.

Facing a possible jail sentence of 45 years, Sanger fled the country. Her brief exile helped shift public attitudes about birth control, as the *New Republic* observed. "We are done with the irresponsible stork," it declared. "We are done with the taboo that forbids discussion of the subject." Sanger returned to a heroine's welcome in 1915, when charges against her were dropped.

She then embarked upon a triumphal speaking tour, where efforts to censor Sanger added yet more allure to her legend. Future ACLU founder Roger Baldwin dated his own engagement with free speech issues to a Sanger speech in St. Louis. Caving to pressure from city officials, the theater where Sanger was supposed to speak turned her away. As an astonished Baldwin looked on, Sanger pounded the locked door amid the cheers of the crowd. The next day, a local newspaper declared that shutting out Sanger had aroused more "popular interest" than her speech would have done.

This pattern was repeated around the country for several years thereafter. When police tried to stop a scheduled Sanger address at New York City's Town Hall in 1921, the crowd lifted her onto the stage while chanting "Defy them! Defy them!" Sanger then announced that she had the right to speak under the Constitution, daring authorities to "club us if they want to." Two officers grabbed her arms and pulled her out of the hall, as the crowd broke into a chorus of "My Country 'Tis of Thee." Sanger was booked on charges of public disorder but released shortly thereafter. The next morning, newspaper accounts of the event placed "birth control"—a formerly taboo term—in bold headlines.

An even stronger stigma was attached to homosexuality, which was referenced obliquely in the press as "deviance," "the sin of Sodom," and so on. The lone exceptions were underground magazines sponsored by gay communities in Los Angeles, New York, and several other large cities.

In 1954, federal authorities confiscated copies of the gay publication *One* on the same grounds that it had censored Margaret Sanger's *The Woman Rebel:* it was obscene. Officials pointed to a short story about a lesbian relationship and a poem alluding to sex between men, which were both held to violate a federal law barring distribution of "lewd and lascivious" materials via the U.S. mails.

A few years later, federal prosecutors charged a gay California businessman with selling photographs of naked men via the mails. Officials also seized copies of a body-building magazine he published, which was popular among male homosexual readers. It wasn't just that gay sex was illegal under state anti-sodomy codes, or that homosexuals were classified by psychiatry as mentally ill. Any discussion of gay themes—including, of course, critiques of gay oppression—could be censored, as well.

But then the Supreme Court intervened, ruling that the Post Office had violated the free speech rights of gay publishers. It drew on changes in obscenity law, which had formerly been used to censor *Ulysses, Lady Chatterley's Lover*, and much else. Courts circumscribed definitions of obscenity after World War II and allowed a much wider berth to novelists, artists, and journalists. And that was a boon for gays and lesbians, who used their new-found First Amendment freedoms to create a dynamic print culture.

Indeed, the homosexual rights movement of the 1960s owes much to gay literature and art, which gave strength to older homosexual communities and galvanized new ones. And none of that could have happened without free-speech protections for gays, which continued to expand in the 1970s and beyond. In 1975, on the eve of the country's 200th birthday, a federal court struck down efforts by the Rhode Island Bicentennial Commission to bar gays from participating in its events. The court ruled that the prohibition unconstitutionally singled out homosexuals, who were endowed with the same right to speak and assemble as any other citizens. It added a jab at the Bicentennial Commission, noting that our Founding Fathers had fought for precisely the free speech rights that the Commission now sought to deny.

That was the same argument invoked by Frederick Douglass in his 1860 address in Boston, the lodestar of the American Revolution. And Black protesters continued to draw upon it across the ensuing century, demanding freedom of speech alongside other rights. When W. E. B. Du Bois and 28 others met in 1905 in Niagara Falls, Canada (because hotels on the American side wouldn't serve Blacks) to form the precursor of the National Association for the Advancement of Colored People (NAACP), they called for free speech as well as access to public facilities and the ballot box. Indeed, Du Bois insisted, African Americans could never gain other civil rights as long as they were prevented from speaking their minds.

After World War II, Du Bois was indicted for being a member of a pacifist organization that authorities deemed "subversive." Although he was acquitted, Du Bois continued to campaign for the free speech rights of others. "It is clear still today, that freedom of speech and of thinking can be attacked in the United States without the intellectual leaders of this land raising a hand or saying a word in protest or defense," Du Bois warned in 1952. "Than this fateful silence there is on earth no greater menace to present civilization."

And as soon as we stop defending free speech, the people with the fewest advantages will suffer. That's what happened at the University of Michigan, which instituted a speech code in 1987 barring "any behavior, verbal or physical, that stigmatizes or victimizes an individual on the basis of race, ethnicity, religion, sex, sexual orientation, creed, national origin, ancestry, age, marital status, handicap, or Vietnam-era veteran status."

Sounds good, right? Wrong. Over the next 18 months, until a federal court struck down the code as unconstitutional, whites charged Blacks with violating it in 20 cases. One African American student was punished for using the term "white trash." I wouldn't call that term racist, but other people saw it differently. And that's the whole point here. When we try to censor speech, even with the best of anti-racist intentions, racial minorities will lose out. And so will the rest of us, because we won't get to hear what they have to say.

We'll also embolden the white racists among us, who want nothing more than to be censored. They have read their history, too, and they know how much appeal they can generate via claims to free speech martyrdom. Attempts to censor John Quincy Adams, Alice Paul, and Margaret Sanger made them into heroes in their respective communities. Do we want to do that for the likes of Richard Spencer and Jared Taylor, the white supremacists who helped organize the infamous 2017 Unite the Right Rally in Charlottesville, Virginia? They already got a boost from President Trump, who said there were "very fine people on both sides" in Charlottesville. The last thing we should do is give them more publicity—and more power—by trying to muzzle them.

Most of all, like all censorship campaigns, the impulse to shut down racist speech reflects a lack of belief in the public itself. Censors see words as viruses, which we need to interdict before they infect the general population. But that's a slight on democracy, which places its faith in the ability of human beings to think, deliberate, and reason.

"No matter to what extent we may disagree with our neighbor, he is entitled to his own opinion," New York Gov. Al Smith declared in 1920, vetoing a law that would have kept Socialists off the ballot in state elections. "It is a confession of the weakness of our own faith in the righteousness of our cause when we attempt to suppress [people] who do not agree with us." The first Catholic to be nominated for president, Smith faced bitter prejudice and hatred because of his religious faith. But his faith in democracy never wavered. Neither should ours.

CHAPTER THREE

Free Speech Allows Us to Create and Enjoy the Art, Film, and Literature of Our Choice

One day, in the late 1970s, I came home from high school carrying a copy of D. H. Lawrence's *Lady Chatterley's Lover*. My father noticed the book and laughed. "I didn't get to read that when I was in school," he said. "Nobody could."

That wasn't exactly right. The book was officially banned from the United States in 1929, under a tariff bill that barred the importation of obscene works. But pirated copies circulated across the country. So did an expurgated version, published in America, which my dad remembered reading at Dartmouth in the early 1950s. "All the good parts got cut out," he joked. He didn't read the full version until the Supreme Court struck down the ban in 1959, when a lot of curious people rushed to purchase it. *Lady Chatterley* shot to number two on *The New York Times* best seller list, topped only by Leon Uris' *Exodus*. Within a year, two million copies had been sold in the United States. My father bought one of them.

All great art is controversial in some way. It challenges our assumptions and makes us look at the world anew. It's also catnip for censors, who generally want to keep things as they are. Almost every classic in literature was prohibited or restricted at some point in our history.

Indeed, in the same year that *Lady Chatterley* was banned, a federal customs inspector declared—only half-facetiously— that "a classic is a dirty book somebody is trying to get by me." Ultimately, however, the censors lost. Thanks to the brave people who stood up for freedom—and, as in the case of *Lady Chatterley*, to the intercession of the courts—you can now read Lawrence, William Faulkner, Ernest Hemingway, and a host of formerly banned authors. You can also watch movies that were deemed obscene in the past, including films by Ingmar Bergman and John Waters.

And, if you so choose, you can consume pornography. That doesn't mean that porn is good for you or for America; depending on the context, it might be neither. But we now have almost unbridled access to it, through the internet, so we the citizens—and not our government—get to decide. That's the American way.

Testifying at a trial in 1990 on behalf of *2 Live Crew*, a rap group charged with obscenity, literary scholar Henry

Louis Gates noted that Shakespeare, Chaucer, and Joyce had also been judged as bawdy and dangerous by authorities in their own times. But in the modern United States, Gates urged, artists and their patrons should have a right to choose what they create and consume.

"One of the hallmarks of a democratic society should be space for all citizens to express themselves in art, whether we like what they have to say or not," Gates wrote in 2010, two decades after the *2 Live Crew* trial. "After all, censorship is to art as lynching is to justice." Censors don't trust us to make up our own minds, any more than a lynch mob trusts a court of law.

The question of censorship is never just about the speech or artwork that is getting squashed. It's about us, and whether we believe we should be free.

America has had many censors, but only one of them had both a law and a noun named after him: Anthony Comstock, the U.S. Postal inspector and activist who fought to purge obscene literature and imagery from the public sphere in the late nineteenth and early twentieth centuries. Shocked by pornography and prostitution in New York, where Comstock moved after serving in the Civil War, he became secretary of the local Society for the Suppression of Vice.

Within a year, Comstock seized more than twelve tons of literature and other risqué items, including photographs, song lyric sheets, playing cards, and (use your imagination) "obscene and immoral rubber articles." He then took his act to

Washington, persuading Congress to pass a federal law barring "obscene, lewd, or lascivious" materials from the U.S. mail.

Known as the Comstock Act, the 1873 measure would be enforced by none other than Anthony Comstock himself. Comstock received a postal inspector's badge and a train pass, allowing him to travel anywhere in America in search of moral contraband. And he found it. By the end of his first year, Comstock had already made 55 arrests; by 1915, when he died, he had helped incarcerate nearly 4,000 perpetrators.

When New York censors stopped George Bernard Shaw's play about prostitution, *Mrs. Warren's Profession*, after a single 1905 performance, Shaw coined a new term for censorship: "Comstockery." Although Comstock himself hadn't been involved in the dispute, the word stuck. To his critics, it signified excessive American prudishness and what Shaw—writing from London—called "the world's standing joke at the expense of the United States." But Comstock happily embraced the term, substituting a more positive definition. Comstockery, he said, was "the applying of the noblest principles of law… in the interest of Public morals, especially those of the young."

Between 1873 and 1915, Comstock seized more than three million pictures and 100,000 pounds of books. He was probably best known for his attacks on contraceptive and sexual information, which brought him head to head with the irrepressible Margaret Sanger and her husband, the architect William Sanger. Comstock forced a Socialist newspaper to drop a 1913 article that Margaret Sanger wrote about venereal disease as part of a series called *What Every Girl Should Know*. After Margaret went abroad to avoid a trial, William was arrested for giving an undercover agent a copy of her book on birth control, *Family Limitation*.

Widely publicized in the press, Comstock's attacks made both Sangers into free speech heroes. "How much longer will liberty-loving men and women submit to 'Comstockery'?" one critic asked. William Sanger was sentenced to thirty days in prison, provoking a storm of protest in the courtroom as an anguished Anthony Comstock looked on. He developed pneumonia and died ten days later, having watched many of his censorship efforts backfire. Whenever Comstock targeted a printed work, a *New York Times* obituary observed, "the controversy was the finest of advertising." As always, the best way to make anything popular in America was to suppress it.

But campaigns against "smut," as the censors called it, continued long after Comstock. In 1920, two female editors of a literary magazine were arrested for publishing an excerpt of James Joyce's *Ulysses* which described a man secretly masturbating while watching a girl. Their lawyer insisted that Joyce's language was too vague to be obscene, prompting a sharp rejoinder from the judge: "The man went off in his pants."

The censorship of Joyce and other prominent authors also produced a backlash in the press, led by the acidic pen of H. L. Mencken. "To be a censor today, a man must be not only an idiot," Mencken wrote in 1924. "He must be also a man courageous enough in his imbecility to endure the low guffaws of his next-door neighbors."

Two years later, in a brilliant piece of performance art, Mencken engineered his own arrest in Boston by selling an issue of *The American Mercury* magazine—which he edited--after local censors banned it for printing a story about a prostitute. A crowd of five thousand followed Mencken to the police station, where he was booked and released. Acquitted by a judge the next day, Mencken proceeded not to prison but to Harvard University, where he received a hero's welcome from 600 students.

Still, Boston's censors were not quite done. The city police chief banned *Scribner's* magazine in 1929 after it serialized Hemingway's *A Farewell to Arms*. That same year, a local bookseller was arrested for selling *Lady Chatterley's Lover*. His shop closed, his wife divorced him, and he sank into alcoholism and died.

But he also became a martyr in the struggle against censorship, which cleverly harnessed satire—alongside indignation—to defend the cause of free expression. Protesters dressed as characters from banned books interrupted a banquet in Ford Hall, circulating a mock petition to prohibit a new novel by author Percy Marks on the grounds that being "Banned in Boston" insured big sales elsewhere. They also staged a skit set in a "Suppressed Book Shop," which refused to sell Grimm's Fairy Tales. "Don't you know that book contains Bolshevik material?" they asked. "Little Red Riding Hood and the Three Little Bears!" Presiding over the event was none other than Margaret Sanger, who sat at a front table wearing a gag over her mouth.

Meanwhile, in the Massachusetts State House a legislator introduced a joke bill requiring censors to "submit to the Department of Health satisfactory evidence of normal sexual experience." In 1930, the state finally amended its obscenity law to end prosecutions of "literary" works.

The quest to censor books gradually took a back seat to a fearsome new challenge: motion pictures. The city of Chicago had passed the nation's first film censorship law in 1907, triggering an avalanche of municipal and state measures around the country. New York's state film law barred material that was "obscene, indecent, immoral, inhuman, sacrilegious or [that] tends to corrupt morals or incite to crime." Not to be outdone, Maryland's censorship board banned "suggestive comedy, stories built on illicit love, over-passionate love scenes, disrespect for the law … men and women living together in adultery without marriage, drinking and gambling made attractive, prolonged success to criminals, maternity scenes, stories and incidents showing disrespect of any religion, advocacy of the doctrine of free love, and titles calculated to stir up racial hatred and antagonistic relations between labor and capital." In other words, everything that interested viewers: sex, violence, and politics.

New York mayor George McClellan, Jr., son of the Civil War general, even tried to close all of the city's nickelodeons— the cheap theaters where movies were shown—on the pretext of fire safety. But the real reason was the same one that motivated censors from time immemorial: the protection of morals, especially those of the young. Smutty films were actually more dangerous than filthy books, Pennsylvania's chief censor warned, because they could be understood by children and also by adults "of the lowest intelligence." That's why the state needed "special agents whose duty it shall be to watch the movies," he added.

And did they ever watch. In 1928, censorship boards around America reviewed 597 feature films, ordering a total of 2,960 cuts in them. More than half of the censored material concerned crime, while a third was connected to sex. Censors in 1933 ordered the removal of a scene showing a woman breast-feeding her child. Other cuts eliminated long kisses, shortening them to pecks, and a scene depicting a dancing girl "shaking her breasts" and "wriggling her body in a suggestive manner." A Memphis review board rejected a film set in a racially integrated classroom, on the grounds that "the South does not permit negroes in white schools nor recognize social equality between the races even in children."

Official censors were joined in their task by the National Board of Review of Motion Pictures, which the film industry formed to stave off the most draconian cuts by state and local authorities. Much depended simply on the taste and the sensibilities of whoever was in charge. "When I became censor in Chicago, I found very little to guide me in the laws of Illinois and the ordinances of Chicago," the city's first movie czar admitted. "The office was too new." A handful of filmmakers challenged censorship on free-speech grounds but found little support in courts, which ruled that movies weren't speech at all. In *Mutual v. Ohio* (1915), the Supreme Court declared that film was "a business, pure and simple," not a form expression. If movies warranted free-speech consideration, the court warned, circuses and billboards might claim the same.

All of that started to change in the 1950s, when courts established new constitutional protections for both literature and film. In *Roth v. United States* (1957), the Supreme Court rejected the idea that the mere depiction of sex made a book obscene. That term should be restricted to publications appealing solely to "prurient interests" and lacking "even the slightest redeeming social importance," the court said. The government could still ban materials in that category. But if a work had any literary or artistic value, it was protected.

A few weeks earlier, San Francisco bookseller Lawrence Ferlinghetti had been arrested for publishing and selling the Allen Ginsberg poem *Howl*, which described (among other taboo subjects) sex between men. The defense team called expert witnesses to testify about the poem's literary merit, as per the *Roth* ruling, and Ferlinghetti was found not guilty.

Two years later, court rulings allowed both the publication of *Lady Chatterley's Lover* (so my father could read it) and even the production of a film based on it. Rejecting censors' claims that the film exposed viewers to "mass sexual immorality," Justice William Douglas said the state could not prohibit materials--in any medium—to guard the public from objectionable ideas. "I can find in the First Amendment no room for any censor whether he is scanning an editorial, reading a news broadcast, editing a novel or a play, or previewing a movie," Douglas wrote. In short, censorship was censorship. The government could not ban movies—any more than books—simply because some official or another didn't like them.

So the censors tried a different tack, stressing harm to to consumers. Congress established a National Commission on

Obscenity and Pornography in 1967, which spent $20 million studying the effects of sexually explicit material on viewers.

In 1970, the panel reported that obscene material wasn't harmful to adults. But others demurred, research be damned. The Senate voted overwhelmingly to repudiate the report, while President Richard Nixon insisted that "the warped and brutal portrayal of sex" in print and film "could poison the wellspring of American and Western culture and civilization."

Two decades later, when Ronald Reagan was in the White House, attorney general Ed Meese established yet another commission on pornography. It successfully pressured the company owning America's 4500 7-11 stores to stop selling *Playboy* and *Penthouse,* although it had less success with other vendors. It also recommended the establishment of a National Obscenity Enforcement Unit in the Justice Department, which targeted mail order distributors. Ignoring a swath of evidence to the contrary, the Meese panel asserted that there was a "causal relationship" between certain kinds of pornography and sexual violence.

So porn wasn't simply a bad idea, which was an insufficient ground for banning it under court doctrine. It promoted bad behavior, especially towards women.

Here the Republican-heavy anti-pornography movement found support from a new and surprising quarter: liberal feminists. Their intellectual leader was law professor Catherine MacKinnon, who started her career as an opponent of censorship. Teaching Yale's first Women's Studies course, she decried Anthony Comstock for persecuting Margret Sanger and others. But she changed her tune in the 1970s, insisting that pornography harmed women.

"Pornography sexualizes rape, battery, sexual harassment, prostitution, and child sexual abuse," MacKinnon wrote. "It thereby celebrates, promotes, authorizes, and legitimates them." MacKinnon helped launch Women Against Pornography, which lobbied for a bill in Minneapolis (her hometown) allowing women to sue producers and distributors of material depicting the "sexually explicit subordination of women."

The measure passed the City Council but was vetoed by the mayor. Five months later, a similar bill was signed into law in Indianapolis. It was challenged in court by bookseller and library associations, which worried that it could be used to censor James Bond movies as well as work by Harold Robbins, Sidney Sheldon, and other pulp-fiction authors. Other opponents included the American Civil Liberties Union, which noted that some literature produced by Woman Against Pornography could itself be held in violation of the law.

A Reagan-appointed female judge ultimately struck down the Indianapolis measure, providing a ringing affirmation of the principles at stake. "Free speech, rather than being the enemy, is a long-tested and worthy ally," she wrote. "To deny free speech in order to engineer social change in the name of accomplishing a greater good for one sector of society erodes the freedom of all."

She was right. Surely, pornography includes many images and themes that degrade women. And like many educators and parents, I'm appalled at the idea of young people—

especially young men—receiving their sexual education from internet porn. But the answer to that problem is to challenge them with different and better materials, not to outlaw the ones that are already there. As the first Chicago film censor admitted, the judgment of what is obscene—and therefore too dangerous for viewers to see—will ultimately come down to the sensibilities of the people doing the censoring. And I don't want state officials telling you—or me—what we should read, listen to, or look at.

This is what happened in Cincinnati in 1990, when an art museum director was arrested for displaying photographs by Robert Mapplethorpe. Some of these photos depicted homoerotic acts, while others showed nude children. After testimony from several witnesses, including parents who confirmed that they had permitted their children to be photographed, the director was acquitted.

But the Corcoran Gallery in Washington cancelled a planned retrospective of Mapplethorpe's work, fearing political backlash. Free-speech advocates projected slides of Mapplethorpe's photos onto the gallery's façade, but nobody got to see the real thing. And that's a loss for art, and for LGBTQ_rights, and for democracy. You don't have to agree with Mapplethorpe's controversial view of the world—including his oft-quoted claim that a picture of a fist up someone's anus isn't much different from one of carnations in a bowl—to acknowledge his profound influence on the visual arts. And, most of all, you can't come to your own conclusion about his work unless you're allowed to see it.

Ditto for artwork containing racially offensive imagery, which has come under fire across America in recent years. In 2019, students and community activists demanded the removal of murals at a San Francisco high school that featured depictions of enslaved African Americans and a slain Native American. Never mind that the painter was a left wing activist who created the murals in the 1930s to protest racism. Today, critics said, the murals threatened harm to the school's minority children.

Sound familiar? The San Francisco censors had no more evidence for that claim than Anthony Comstock did in his paeans to protecting the young from immorality. They simply wanted to impose their morality on somebody else, which is the essence of censorship in all times and places.

Ironically, some of the same people demanding removal of the murals wanted to re-name the school after African American novelist Maya Angelou, one of its most distinguished alumnae. But Angelou was herself a frequent target of censorship as well as a tireless critic of it. Her 1969 book *I Know Why the Caged Bird Sings* remains one of the most frequently banned books in American schools and libraries, sparking controversy because of its frank depictions of rape, homosexuality, and racism. One parent of an African American student in Arizona even filed suit to block her school from assigning the book, on the grounds that it would cause "psychological injuries" among young Black readers.

Fortunately, a federal court turned away the lawsuit. If Angelou's memoir could be removed because it offended Black students, the court said, Jewish students might block works by Shakespeare, female students might seek a ban on Freud, and male students might attempt to censor Margaret Atwood. As

Maya Angelou wrote in 2009, in a poem commemorating the 40th anniversary of *I Know Why the Caged Bird Sings*, censors can find something offensive in almost anything:

> *They were scared of sexes and hexes*
> *and multi-colored sheets.*
> *And men and women doing even*
> *consensual things.*
> *They banned a same-sex marriage room*
> *and Judy Blume*
> *Charles Dickens Chicken-Lickin and*
> *Why the Caged Bird Sings*

CHAPTER FOUR

Free Speech Allows Students and Teachers to Speak Their Minds at School

I n 2018, after a shooter murdered fourteen people at a high school in Parkland, Florida, student protests engulfed the United States. Thousands of young people walked out of school or staged demonstrations inside of them, demanding stronger gun control measures. A journalist called me to ask what was new about this outburst of student activism.

"Nothing," I said. "What's new is that the adults are embracing it."

This has not been the case for most of American history. Like wartime dissent, which was highly restricted by government authorities, "student rights" were minimal or non-existent prior to the 1960s. It's rare to find mention of that term before the civil rights struggle, which brought it into the popular lexicon.

The movement for racial justice in the United States was also a youth movement, enlisting thousands of teenagers and young adults in sit-ins, marches, and other forms of protest. So it inevitably seeped into high schools, where African American students denounced segregation and other forms of white supremacy. That paved the way for multi-racial protests against the war in Vietnam, which spread like wildfire through America's classrooms and corridors.

School officials did everything they could to tamp down the protesters, but they ultimately failed, thanks in large part to the intercession of the Supreme Court. In its landmark 1969 decision, *Tinker v. Des Moines*, the court famously ruled that neither students nor teachers "shed their constitutional rights to freedom of speech or expression at the schoolhouse gate."

Since the 1980s, court doctrine has placed new limits on what both groups can say in school. But surely students and teachers have vastly more liberty to speak their minds than they did during prior eras.

And that's a good thing, for all of us. Especially at our present moment of political polarization, which has clogged the airwaves with constant snark and invective, our future citizens need to learn a better way to speak across their differences. They won't be able to do that if students—and their teachers—are blocked from addressing the questions that divide us.

Of course, our young people should be allowed to raise their voices on the question of guns, and everything else. But the real question is what kind of adults we want them to become. They will never learn to discuss controversial issues in a mutually respectful manner if we purge these issues from our classrooms.

In 1964, Black students at a segregated high school in Philadelphia, Mississippi were suspended for wearing "freedom buttons" adorned with the phrase "One Man One Vote" and the acronym "SNCC," which stood for the Student Nonviolent Coordinating Committee. The school was near the site of the murder of three civil rights workers who had been trying to register Black Americans to vote, in defiance of longtime laws and practices that had disenfranchised them.

So tensions in the area were running high. The principal suspended about fifty students, sending them home with a note informing their parents that "it is against school policy for anything to be brought into the school that is not educational."

In fact, other students had worn his-and-her "going steady" buttons as well as pins celebrating the Beatles, who had toured the country earlier that year. But the principal insisted that the school had the right to decide what students could wear, and a local judge agreed. "If children are permitted to go through the lower grades running the school, rather than teachers running the children, it will probably wind up in a lot of juvenile delinquency," the judge wrote, rejecting the students' plea for an injunction against their suspensions.

The following winter, at a second segregated Mississippi high school, another group of Black students wore SNCC buttons to school. Instructed by their African American principal to remove the buttons, they asked him if he had registered to vote. They also called him an "Uncle Tom," claiming he was kowtowing to white authority. The button-

wearing movement grew to 300 students, a third of the student population, who were suspended a week after it began. It then spread to three other schools in two counties, where roughly a thousand students boycotted classes for the rest of the academic year.

As in the first button case, the students sued for an injunction on First Amendment grounds and were turned away by a local judge, who deemed the matter "a disciplinary problem" rather than a free speech issue. But on appeal, in 1965 a federal circuit court ruled that the "freedom button" communicated "a matter of vital public concern." So it was also protected speech, provided that it did not interfere with the daily functioning and "decorum" of school.

Four years later, that distinction became the centerpiece of *Tinker v. Des Moines*, when the Supreme Court ruled that students could express their opinions as long as they did not threaten "substantial disruption" of school activities. At issue were three teenagers who had worn black armbands to school to protest America's war in Vietnam.

Significantly, all three were from families with roots in the civil rights struggle. John and Mary Beth Tinker, who became the lead plaintiffs in the case, had moved to Des Moines, Iowa after their father, a Methodist minister, was pushed out of his previous assignment for endorsing Blacks' right to use the town swimming pool. The third plaintiff, Christopher Eckhardt, had accompanied his parents to civil rights marches and had met activist author John Howard Griffin, author of the protest memoir *Black Like Me*.

The three students were sent home from school in December 1965, and told that they could not return if they continued to wear the armbands. All of them went back after the Christmas break wearing black clothes instead of armbands; in fact, John Tinker would wear black every day until the end of the school year.

Some members of the community offered them quiet support. But vandals threw red paint at the Tinker home, which also received a bomb threat, while Christopher Eckhardt's parents got hate mail accusing them of harming their son by supporting his armband protest. "Your [sic] going to have a Harvey Lee Oswald on your hands," one letter-writer charged, butchering the name of John F. Kennedy's assassin (as well as the contraction for "you are").

Meanwhile, with the assistance of the ACLU, the three students sued the school district on free speech grounds. They lost at the district and circuit court levels but prevailed in the Supreme Court, where Christopher Eckhardt, Mary Beth Tinker and their parents looked on anxiously while the justices deliberated their fate. (John Tinker had fallen asleep in Iowa waiting for his plane and missed the hearing.)

The school district argued that the armband protest threatened the "scholarly atmosphere" of area public schools, which were already inflamed by the recent death of a Des Moines student in Vietnam. But upon questioning by Justice Thurgood Marshall, the district admitted that only seven of its 18,000 students had worn armbands. When Marshall's eyelids started to droop later in the argument, the Tinkers recalled, they knew they had won.

In a ringing decision, Justice Abe Fortas flatly declared that students "are entitled to freedom of expression" while in schools. "In our system, state-operated schools may not be enclaves of totalitarianism," Fortas added. "Students may not be regarded as closed-circuit recipients of only that which the State chooses to communicate." Drawing on the button cases from Mississippi, Fortas noted that schools could restrict speech if they could show that it would "materially and substantially interfere" with day-to-day operations. Otherwise, students must be free to say what they thought.

The case triggered a blistering dissent from Justice Hugo Black, who warned that it signaled "a new revolutionary era of permissiveness in this country fostered by the judiciary." He was wrong. *Tinker* proved to be the high-water mark for student rights in the United States, which have been slowly scaled back since then.

In 1986, the Supreme Court upheld the suspension of a student who used sexual innuendo ("he's firm in his pants") in a nominating speech for a friend who was running for student government. And in 2007, it also upheld a school's suspension of a student for displaying a banner that read "Bong Hits for Jesus" outside the school building.

Neither decision claimed that the speech in question threatened material disruption, as per the *Tinker* standard. Instead, the courts decreed that the content of the speech was inappropriate in an educational setting—and, most of all, that officials had both the right and the duty to enforce such standards in school. The Bong Hits banner was "reasonably viewed as promoting illegal drug use," Chief

Justice John Roberts wrote, so it was reasonable for the school to censor it.

And surely reasonable people can and do disagree about these matters. Is it OK for schools to prohibit students from wearing T-shirts showing aborted fetuses? How about Confederate flags? Or shirts quoting passages from the Bible that have been interpreted as condemning homosexuality?

All of these dilemmas have confronted school officials in the post-*Tinker* era. Most recently, an Oregon school sent a student home for wearing a shirt bearing the words "Donald J. Trump Border Wall Construction Co." and "The Wall Just Got 10 Feet Taller." The district argued that the T-shirt could have caused racially motivated disruptions at the school, where one-third of the students were Latino and some had family members who were deported. The T-shirt wearer countered that many other people at the school had displayed anti-Trump messages without incident, so the school should also allow a pro-Trump one.

These are tough calls, requiring delicate balancing acts between students' First Amendment rights and the school's wish to maintain a safe educational environment. But almost nobody on either side of these debates asserted that students had no rights, which was generally the case before *Tinker*. In that sense, even the quest for "balance" in these cases shows us how deeply student free speech rights have become inscribed in contemporary American life.

This is not the case for teacher speech, unfortunately, which has been much more circumscribed in recent years. Like free speech in the country as a whole, the rights of teachers have usually narrowed when the nation goes to war.

In the buildup to the Civil War, as communities and states sought to censor anti-slavery literature, school boards likewise dismissed teachers suspected of harboring "abolitionist" views. One Virginia newspaper even suggested that these instructors should be assassinated "for poisoning the minds of our slaves or our children." The safest bet was for teachers to avoid the slavery issue and every other controversial question, as leaders of America's burgeoning common-school movement urged.

"If the day ever arrives when the school room shall become a cauldron for the fermentation of all the hot and virulent opinions, in politics and religion, that now agitate our community, that day the fate of our glorious public school system will be sealed, and speedy ruin will overwhelm it," warned Horace Mann, America's best-known champion of common schools. An ardent foe of slavery, Mann nevertheless worried that parents would withdraw support from schools that discussed it. "The moment it is known or supposed that the [school] cause is to be perverted to, or connected with, any of the exciting party questions of the day, I shall never get another cent," Mann predicted.

The atmosphere shifted during the early twentieth century, when avowedly "progressive" educators like John Dewey called upon schools to engage the central public questions of their time. Hundreds of districts introduced current-events lessons, requiring students to bring in newspaper articles and present them in class.

But these conversations were severely restricted upon America's entry into World War I, when teachers were disciplined for raising doubts about the conflict. One New York City teacher was dismissed for telling his class that pacifists should be allowed to visit schools alongside military recruiters, so students hear "both sides." Another told students that he "was not allowed to tell the truth to his pupils," which was confirmed when he, too, was fired.

Teachers received slightly more leeway amid the Great Depression during the 1930s, leading debates about the causes of the crisis and the "New Deal" of federal programs that aimed to remedy it. But they faced new constraints during World War II and especially the Cold War, when hundreds of teachers were fired for prior or present-day affiliations with the Communist Party. In that climate, raising any political question at all could also raise the specter of disloyalty.

"Every teacher knows that controversial issues are almost taboo in our schools today," an attorney for three fired teachers observed. "Teachers will tell you, with not a happy smile, 'I just do not discuss anything more controversial than the weather anymore.'" A *Washington Post* columnist put the matter more succinctly: "School teachers are like the Sphinx," he noted. "They seldom express their own views."

The accordion widened somewhat in the 1960s, when some teachers divulged their opinions about civil rights and the war in Vietnam. But others lost their jobs for doing so, especially in more conservative parts of the country.

In 1970, just a year after *Tinker*, five Indiana teachers were fired for wearing armbands to school in protest of the war. A school board in Wyoming dismissed three teachers for playing soundtracks to *Hair* and *Alice's Restaurant* in class, as part of a lesson about anti-war protest. "In a small community," a court declared, upholding their dismissal, "the Board members and principal surely have a right to emphasize a more orthodox approach."

Federal courts did reinstate a Texas history teacher in 1980 who had been fired for using a simulation game in which students played different racial groups in the community. But most teachers continued to eschew controversy in their classrooms, especially on matters related to race and sex. One Virginia health teacher reported that her school's rules blocked her from addressing questions that her students had generated, including the location of the nearest venereal disease clinic. Nor could she discuss ethical issues they had raised, such as the appropriate age of consent and whether a student who became pregnant should tell her parents.

When the U.S. invaded Iraq in 2003, finally, teachers faced an all-too-predictable set of constraints. Two teachers in New Mexico were suspended for hanging posters in their classrooms urging "No War in Iraq," which the district said violated the school's policy against "indoctrination."

And surely that is a danger in any educational setting, where teachers should be free to state their opinions yet must make sure not to force these views upon students. But other parts of the school were festooned with military recruiting posters, which were not taken to violate the policy. Clearly, then, the New Mexico teachers were being disciplined for what they believed rather than for imposing those beliefs on the young people in their charge.

In 2007, a federal court upheld an Indiana school board that decided not to renew a teacher's contract after she told her class—in response to a student question—that she opposed the Iraq war. The constitution "does not entitle primary and secondary teachers ... to advocate viewpoints that depart from the curriculum," the court held. "Students ... ought not to be subject to teachers' idiosyncratic perspectives."

But how can students learn the skills of democracy *unless* teachers are allowed to share their own perspectives? Of course, teachers should not be required to say what they think, about the Iraq War or anything else. But surely they should be *allowed* to do so, as long as students understand that they are not required to echo their teachers' point of view.

This became ever more imperative with the election of Donald Trump, which triggered angry recrimination and name-calling across the land. To counter that trend, we need teachers to model a different style of discourse. And they can't do that if they have to pretend that they are neutral figures, standing above the fray, instead of political actors in their own right.

"It is obvious that the teacher must be free to do what he is trying to get his students to do," philosopher Alexander Meiklejohn wrote in 1938, denouncing school districts for muzzling teachers. "To require our teachers to say to their pupils, 'I want you to learn from me how to do what I am forbidden to do,' is to make of education the most utter nonsense."

Have some teachers abused their power in the classroom? Of course. During the 2016 election, an Arkansas teacher resigned after calling outgoing president Barack Obama a "monkey." He also told his class that Obama had been born in Kenya, echoing the "birther" lie promoted by Trump and many others. Obviously, such racist drivel has no place in our schools. But nor does calling President Trump's supporters "Nazis" or "fascists," which has gotten other teachers in trouble—and appropriately so—around the country.

Teachers have no business vilifying an entire category of voters, any more than they should slur people on the basis of their race. Their job is to help students come to their own conclusions, about Trump and everything else. And, most of all, it's to teach our young people how to resolve their differences in a civil and mutually respectful manner. We'll never improve the poor quality of speech in America if we don't allow our teachers—and their students—to speak their minds in school.

Free Speech in the Age of COVID-19 and Black Lives Matter

I wrote most of this book in late 2019, putting the finishing touches on it—or so I imagined—in January 2020.

Just a few weeks later, news started to emerge about a dangerous virus that had stricken Wuhan, China. Then a nursing home in Washington State reported an outbreak of the same pathogen, which spread quickly to every corner of our country. Seeking to slow the rate of infection, state governments ordered businesses, schools, and most other institutions to close their doors. But by April, more than 40,000 Americans had died of COVID-19, the novel coronavirus; three months later, the deaths toll surpassed 150,000. By the time this book appears, an untold number of others will also have perished.

In the darker corners of the internet, meanwhile, a very different story was being spread about COVID-19. It was hatched in a laboratory by evil Chinese scientists who conspired with members of the "Deep State" here in the United States— or with Bill Gates, or with George Soros—to inflict a deadly disease on all of us. Others claimed that the entire crisis was a hoax, cooked up by enemies of President Trump to destroy the economy and derail his re-election bid in November 2020.

In April, as death tolls continued to mount, thousands of protesters converged on state capitols across the country to denounce stay-at-home orders and demand the restoration of their God-given freedoms. They carried American flags, small children, and—in several locations—semi-automatic rifles. And they were egged on by none other than Donald J. Trump, who tweeted his support for "liberation" from the lockdown measures that his own scientific advisers had recommended.

It's tempting to argue that this kind of irresponsible speech should be banned, even when—or, perhaps, especially when—the president of the United States is spouting it. And censoring it is quite popular, as a March 2020 survey confirmed. Interviewing a nationally representative sample of 3,000 Americans, researchers found that roughly 70 percent of them favored "restricting people's ability to say things that may qualify as misinformation" during the coronavirus crisis. And while Democrats and Republicans differed radically in their approval of President Trump's handling of the pandemic, they were equally supportive of measures to muzzle false statements about it. "Red and Blue America Agree That Now is the Time to Violate the Constitution," one headline declared, reporting the results of the survey.

Surprised? You shouldn't be. The survey confirmed our long-standing and bipartisan penchant for stamping out dangerous speech, especially during national emergencies. Indeed, as Oliver Wendell Holmes noted almost exactly a century ago, it is "perfectly logical" to censor rebels and malcontents at moments like this. When there's a war going on, why should we let someone play for the other team? Doesn't that portend a kind of national suicide? We need to protect ourselves, and we need to win. So dissidents should be silenced, at least until the war is over.

No. A thousand times no. If any single lesson emerges from our lengthy and tortured history of censorship, it's that censorship never works. It gives fuel and ammunition to its targets, who get free publicity when their free speech is violated. And it sets up the censors to be censored themselves once a new sheriff comes to town.

Recall that the *Nation* magazine led the charge to muzzle fascists like William Dudley Pelley during World War II. But when the hot war against Nazism gave way to the cold war against Communism, the *Nation* was removed from libraries and schools because of its supposedly "Red" slant. If you believe in free speech, you have to guarantee it for everyone. Full stop. And when you start to make exceptions, watch out! The next time, the censors may be coming for you.

Sadly, we keep forgetting that lesson so we have to re-learn it, over and over again. In March 2020, as the coronavirus lockdowns began, the public safety director in Newark, New Jersey released a statement warning that spreading misinformation about the virus could result in criminal prosecution. "Individuals who make any false or baseless reports about the coronavirus in Newark can set off a domino effect that can result in injury to residents and visitors and affect schools, houses of worship, businesses, and entire neighborhoods," the statement declared. "New Jersey has laws regarding a false public alarm and we will enforce those laws."

In the U.S. territory of Puerto Rico, the governor signed a security measure making it illegal for media outlets or individuals to transmit "false information with the intention of creating confusion, panic, or public hysteria" surrounding COVID-19. Never mind that similar laws were used in China to punish coronavirus whistleblowers like Wuhan physician Li Wenliang, who was summoned by authorities in the middle of the night and forced to confess to making "false comments."

Li's warnings went unheeded, which allowed the virus to spread more rapidly and to claim thousands of lives—including his own. Censors always think they have a monopoly on truth, of course, which seemingly gives them both the right and the responsibility to purge everything that's false from the public square.

Yet that is a delusion and a falsehood in its own right. Granted, many claims made by the anti-lockdown protesters run counter to the best knowledge and practice of scientists, including those who were providing guidance to President Trump. Yet scientists don't know everything. And in the past, pressure from the public has exposed their blind spots and forced them to change.

Dr. Anthony Fauci, President Trump's most prominent scientific adviser, is justly lauded as one of the heroes of the fight against HIV/AIDS. But in the early stages of that epidemic, he was reviled by AIDS activists an "incompetent idiot" and even as a "murderer" (yes, you can look it up) because he insisted that drugs in clinical trials must be proven to be effective before they were given to AIDS patients. Activists persuaded him that people who were dying should have access to any drug that was shown to be safe, even if its effectiveness had not yet been established in trials. As a result, thousands of people who otherwise might have succumbed to AIDS got a new lease on life.

Earlier in his career, Fauci would not have listened to loudmouthed laypeople telling him how to do his job. "There was a feeling in science that doctors know best, scientists know best," Fauci recalled in a 2020 interview. "We love our patients, but they don't really know what's best for them." Fauci listened, and he learned. And we are all the better for it.

Let me be clear. In no way am I equating the courageous activists of the AIDS battle to the charlatans and conspiracy theorists who are protesting the coronavirus lockdowns. Nor do I believe that these protesters have a "right" to flout social distancing guidelines and place other people at physical risk, any more than I have a right to drive at 100 miles an hour while I'm drunk. But they *do* have the right to denounce the restrictions and to criticize government officials, including scientists like Anthony Fauci.

It's absurd to censor their speech on the grounds that it might prompt dangerous behavior, which is another recurring fallacy in the censorship playbook. In his *Schenck* ruling, which Oliver Wendell Holmes subsequently regretted, Holmes worried that leaflets urging draft resistance might harm America's ability to fight—and win—World War I. Indeed, he said that they were tantamount to falsely shouting fire in a theater. They weren't. The shouting-fire argument betrays a curious lack of faith in the judgment of the public, even as it claims to protect that same public from the evil effects of bad speech.

As of this writing, the vast majority of Americans continue to support stay-at-home orders and other measures to restrict the spread of COVID-19. If anything, it would seem, protest against these measures has stiffened our resolve to retain them. Censoring the demonstrators would most likely have the opposite effect, amplifying their message and drawing more people into their camp.

It would also deprive the rest of us of the chance to hear them, and—yes—to learn from them. In a democracy, it's important to know how your fellow citizens feel. And they might have something important to say about our society, even if they are radically distorting our science. Why should a Walmart be allowed to sell flowers, for example, while local florists are shut down as "nonessential" businesses? Why is it OK for people to gather on a municipal bus, but not at a public school? The question of when and how to "re-open" our economy is extraordinarily complex, touching on our deepest conceptions of ourselves as family members, workers, consumers, and Americans.

We should let everyone speak, even when—or especially when—it repulses us. It won't be pretty, but it's better than the alternative. Winston Churchill said that democracy is the worst form of government, except for all of the others. Ditto for free speech. It's messy and ugly and contentious, but it sure beats letting someone else tell you what you're allowed to say.

The censors now include big social media platforms, especially Facebook, which took down posts by some of the organizers of the anti-lockdown protests. Its rationale echoed the shouting-fire defense in Holmes' *Schenck* ruling: When content poses "risk of imminent physical harm," CEO Mark Zuckerberg said Facebook removes it. "Certainly, someone saying that social distancing is not effective to help limit the spread of coronavirus, we do classify that as harmful misinformation and we take that down," Zuckerberg explained. "At the same time, it's important that people can debate policies."

But how can that debate take place, in a full and free fashion, if Facebook is deciding what is "harmful" and what is not? Shouldn't that be up to the reader? To be sure, Facebook is a private company; unlike the government, it can "censor" anything it wants. But as an American Civil Liberties Union official argued, it also wields enormous power over its billion or so users. It "should not be censoring political speech," the ACLU official said, particularly at a moment "when questions of when and how to reopen the country are among the central political questions, and online platforms are the main vehicle for expression."

It would be better were Facebook to add its own messages to false and misleading content, on the principle that the best solution to misinformation is always better information. Facebook wisely placed links to the Center for Disease Control guidelines on some of the anti-lockdown protest pages, which was a much smarter move than taking down the other pages.

Indeed, Facebook's efforts to gag anti-lockdown protesters sparked a loud and predictable protest of its own. It was led by Donald Trump, Jr., the president's son, who gleefully took up the cudgel of civil liberties against the big bad censor. "Why is @Facebook colluding with state governments to quash peoples [sic] free speech?" Trump, Jr. tweeted. "Regardless of what you think about the lockdown or the protests against them, this is a chilling and disturbing government directed shutdown of peoples [sic] First Amendment rights. Very dangerous!"

Despite his poor spelling—and despite his baseless claim that state governments had "directed" Facebook's actions—Trump, Jr. had a point. And it wasn't lost on his father, either, who was similarly reborn as a tribune of unfettered dialogue and exchange. "These people are expressing their views," President Trump said, praising the protesters. "They seem to be very responsible people to me."

Never mind that some of these "responsible people" were wielding AR-15s at statehouse rallies, or that Trump has repeatedly called for the censorship of his own critics. Just a few days before he praised the protesters, in fact, Trump's re-election campaign sent a cease-and-desist letter to television stations that aired an advertisement attacking his weak response to the coronavirus. Citing alleged inaccuracies in the ad, an attorney for the campaign warned that stations showing it could lose their broadcast licenses.

This was nothing new for the president, who had earlier suggested that the Federal Communications Commission consider removing the licenses of MSNBC and CNN because of their so-called "fake news" attacks on him. (Never mind that both news outlets are cable channels—not over-the-air broadcasters—so the FCC doesn't license them.) But the answer to a censorship-happy president is never to censor him or his supporters, which simply reinforces the idea that dangerous speech must be suppressed.

At the same time that the Trump campaign was threatening the licenses of stations that ran attacks on him, an anti-Trump advocacy group—ironically called "Free Press"—charged that the president was "spreading misinformation" about hydroxychloroquine as a possible treatment for coronavirus. The group was right about Trump's claims, which vastly exaggerated what we know about the drug's efficacy. But it was wrong to demand that the FCC investigate the spread of this information by the president and his allies via broadcast outlets, which sounded a lot like Trump's calls for the agency to examine "fake news" against him.

Just as two wrongs never make a right, it is always wrong to censor another party simply because it tried to censor you. An eye for an eye in these matters makes the whole world blind—or at least, intensely cynical—about free speech itself.

So have the myriad attacks on free speech since the death of George Floyd in May 2020, which sparked one of the largest bouts of protest in U.S. history. Proclaiming that "Black Lives Matter," millions of Americans took to the streets to demand justice for Floyd and other victims of police brutality. In response, police too often brutalized the demonstrators themselves. In Charleston, South Carolina, officers arrested a Black man who dropped to one knee and told them, "All of you are my family." In Kansas City, they arrested another African American who shouted from a crowd that police should "turn in their damned badge" if they failed to "protect and serve" the public.

When journalists tried to hold police to account, they faced threats of their own. By July 2020, more than 500 reporters had suffered aggressions by police and more than 70 had been arrested.

Unsurprisingly, some of the most brazen attacks on free speech came from the Trump administration. Federal officers used tear gas and rubber bullets to clear a peaceful protest across from the White House, all so President Trump could pose for a photo-op while holding a Bible. And Trump dispatched federal forces to Portland, Oregon, where officers employed unmarked vehicles to detain demonstrators. "The use of unidentified military forces against the wishes of local officials, the exercise of excessive force against peaceful demonstrators and the seemingly arbitrary detention of some of them without a clear reason for arrest are designed to intimidate protesters into surrendering their First Amendment rights," a coalition of civil-liberties groups warned.

Yet some of the same people protesting Trump and police brutality exercised their own brand of intimidation to squelch free speech. Their weapons were not tanks and guns but Twitter and Instagram, which were used to vilify, demean, and bully (or "cancel," in today's vernacular) anyone who dared question the protest movement. A respected reporter was flayed for quoting an African American about Black victims of crime, which supposedly diverted needed attention from police brutality; a data scientist at a progressive think tank was fired for circulating a study showing that urban rioting helped conservative candidates at the polls; and growing numbers of Americans told researchers that they were afraid to express their opinions, lest they suffer retaliation at work and ostracism by their peers.

Meanwhile, echoing the San Francisco high school dispute, the University of Kentucky announced that it would remove a 1930s-era mural that had drawn social media denunciations over its depiction of slavery. It mattered little that the university had commissioned noted African American artist Karyn Olivier in 2018 to create an installation to counter the mural, or that Olivier firmly opposed taking it down. "The day I completed my response to the mural was the day the university's real work needed to begin," Olivier wrote. "Instead, removing the mural chooses silence, erasure, and avoidance over engagement, investigation, and real reconciliation. Is the hope that we'll simply forget our shared history?"

To be clear, there is a huge difference between unidentified federal officers arresting a protester and a university removing a piece of offending artwork. But they share the same illiberal spirit, which is the enemy of free speech everywhere. That was the theme of a letter released by more than 150 prominent authors and artists in July 2020, who warned that a pall of censorship was descending across the nation.

"The restriction of debate, whether by a repressive government or an intolerant society, invariably hurts those who lack power and makes everyone less capable of democratic participation," the letter declared. "We refuse any false choice between justice and freedom, which cannot exist without each other." The letter was signed by more than two dozen people of color, including Salman Rushdie, Wynton Marsalis, and Fareed Zakaria. Other signatories included Margaret Atwood, J. K. Rowling, and University of Chicago economist Deirdre McCloskey, a trans woman.

None of this prevented indignant critics from denouncing the letter as a defense of "the intellectual freedom of cis white intellectuals," which "has never been under threat en masse." But censorship threatens all of us, and—like a cancer—it grows larger when we ignore it. In dismissing the letter as a ploy by privileged cisgendered whites, critics slighted the racial and sexual minorities who had signed it. They also reinforced the spirit of suppression and intolerance, which are never far from the surface in American life.

But aren't there some ideas—especially racist, sexist, and homophobic ones—that *should* be suppressed? Why should we tolerate speech that is itself intolerant?

We shouldn't, if that means keeping quiet. All of us should raise our voices against the bigotries, prejudices, and hatreds that continue to afflict our country. That's an exercise of free speech in its own right, and it has been crucial to campaigns for social justice from abolitionism and women's suffrage right up to Black Lives Matter.

But speaking up is different from denying speech to someone else, which never ends well. As we have seen in these pages, censorship makes its targets into martyrs. Instead of muzzling their ideas, it gives them more power and allure. It also betrays a curious lack of confidence in democracy itself. If we truly believe in our ability to govern ourselves, we need to let every citizen speak their mind. And we need to have faith that this cacophony of voices will yield a more just and fair society than any set of censors could possibly create.

Americans have kept that faith, even in these dark times. The COVID-19 outbreak and the George Floyd protests highlighted threats to free speech, to be sure, but they also reminded us how deeply it is woven into the fabric of the nation. Local officials condemned police who harassed Black Lives Matter protesters, while city and state leaders around the country blasted the Trump administration for its military-style clampdown on the largely peaceful Portland demonstrations. Several governors also took pains to express their support for the speech rights of anti-lockdown protesters, even as officials pleaded with them to maintain social distancing.

"It's OK to be frustrated. It's OK to be angry," Michigan governor Gretchen Whitmer said, after protesters swarmed her state capitol to denounce coronavirus-related restrictions. "If it makes you (feel) better to direct it at me, that's OK, too. I've got a thick skin. And I'm always going to defend your right to free speech." Likewise, California governor Gavin Newsom reiterated protesters' right to criticize him. "I just want to encourage people, when you practice your free speech—which I don't embrace, I celebrate—just do so safely," Newsom urged. "This virus knows no political ideology."

Neither does freedom of speech. It's for all of us, no matter what might divide us. An attack on one American's free speech is an attack on everyone's. "Liberty is meaningless where the right to utter one's thoughts and opinions has ceased to exist," Frederick Douglass told a Boston audience in 1860, on the eve of the Civil War. "There can be no right of speech where any man, however lifted up, or however humble, however young, or however old, is overawed by force, and compelled to suppress his honest sentiments." As a former slave, Douglass knew vastly more about the brutalities and inequalities of America than did most of his listeners. But he also knew that we could never make anything right if we forsook the right to free speech.

At another moment of grave national crisis, we need to unite behind this quintessential American tradition. It has been bruised and battered, to be sure, but it remains the best way to bridge our innumerable differences.

Let free speech ring! Anything less will diminish us all.

A Brief Bibliography

Ball, Carlos A. *The First Amendment and LGBT Equality: A Contentious History.* Cambridge: Harvard, 2017.

Bollinger, Lee C. and Geoffrey R. Stone, eds. *The Free Speech Century.* New York: Oxford, 2019.

Curtis, Michael Kent. *Free Speech, "The People's Darling Privilege": Struggles for Freedom of Expression in American History.* Durham: Duke, 2000.

Driver, Justin. *The Schoolhouse Gate: Public Education, the Supreme Court, and the Battle for the American Mind.* New York: Pantheon, 2018.

Dubin, Steven C. *Arresting Images: Impolitic Art and Uncivil Actions.* New York: Routledge, 1992.

Engelman, Peter C. *A History of the Birth Control Movement in America*. Santa Barbara: Praeger, 2011.

Finan, Christopher M. *From the Palmer Raids to the Patriot Act: A History of the Fight for Free Speech in America.* Boston: Beacon, 2007.

Geltzer, Jeremy. *Dirty Words and Filthy Pictures: Film and the First Amendment.* Austin: University of Texas, 2015.

Gunther, Gerald. *Learned Hand: The Man and the Judge.* New York: Oxford, 2010.

Johnson, John W. *The Struggle for Student Rights: Tinker v. Des Moines and the 1960s.* Lawrence: University Press of Kansas, 1997.

Mackinnon, Catherine and Andrea Dworkin, eds. *In Harm's Way: The Pornography Civil Rights Hearings.* Cambridge: Harvard, 1997.

Ross, Catherine J. *Lessons in Censorship: How Schools and Courts Subvert Students' First Amendment Rights.* Cambridge: Harvard, 2015.

Schumaker, Kathryn. *Troublemakers: Students' Rights and Racial Justice in the Long 1960s.* New York: New York University, 2019.

Smith, Craig ed. S*ilencing the Opposition: How the United States Government Suppressed Freedom of Expression During Major Crises.* Albany: SUNY, 2011.

Stone, Geoffrey R. *Perilous Times: Free Speech in Wartime.* New York: Norton, 2004.

Strossen, Nadine. *Hate: Why We Should Resist It With Free Speech, Not Censorship*. New York: Oxford, 2018.

Werbel, Amy. *Lust on Trial: Censorship and the Rise of Obscenity in the Age of Anthony Comstock*. New York: Columbia, 2018.

Zimmerman, Jonathan. *Campus Politics: What Everyone Needs to Know*. New York: Oxford, 2016.

Zimmerman, Jonathan and Emily Robertson. *The Case for Contention: Teaching Controversial Issues in American Schools*. Chicago: University of Chicago, 2017.

Index

A

abolitionists, 21–23, 50, 61–62, 79

Abrams v. United States, 10

Adams, John, 4, 5

Adams, John Quincy, 23, 32

African Americans. *See* Black people

AIDS activists, 71–72

Alice's Restaurant recording, 63

Alien and Sedition Acts, 4–5

American Civil Liberties Union (ACLU), 26, 47, 58, 74

The American Mercury magazine, 41

Angelou, Maya, 50–51

Anthony, Susan B., xii

anti-slavery movement, 21–23, 50, 61–62, 79

anti-war sentiment and protests, x–xii, 2–3, 13, 54, 57–58, 63

Arizona, 50

Arkansas, 65

armbands, 57–59, 63

art and artists, 35–51, 79–80

Ashcroft, John, 16

Atwood, Margaret, 80

authors, banned, 35–36

B

Baldwin, Roger, 26, 28

banned books, 35–36, 50–51

Bill of Rights, 26

birth control and contraception, 27–29, 39, 40

"birther" lie, 65

Black, Hugo, 13, 59

Black Like Me (Griffin), 57

Black Lives Matter movement, 77–79, 81

Jonathan Zimmerman

The Amateur Hour: A History of College Teaching in America (Johns Hopkins University Press, 2020)

The Case for Contention: Teaching Controversial Issues in American Schools, co-authored with Emily Robertson (University of Chicago Press, 2017)

Campus Politics: What Everyone Needs to Know (Oxford University Press, 2016)

Too Hot to Handle: A Global History of Sex Education (Princeton University Press, 2015)

Small Wonder: The Little Red Schoolhouse in History and Memory (Yale University Press, 2009)

Innocents Abroad: American Teachers in the American Century (Harvard University Press, 2006)

Whose America? Culture Wars in the Public Schools (Harvard University Press, 2002)

Distilling Democracy: Alcohol Education in America's Public Schools, 1880-1925 (University Press of Kansas, 1999)

Signe Wilkinson

Herstory: 19 Cartoons in Celebration of the 19th Amendment (2019)

One Nation, Under Surveillance: Cartoon Rants on Life, Liberty and the Pursuit of Privacy (Cartoonist Group, 2005)

Abortion Cartoons on Demand (Broad Street Books, 1992)

Wilkinson's cartoons have also appeared in many collections, including *Drawn to Purpose: American Women Illustrators and Cartoonists*, by Martha H. Kennedy for the Library of Congress (University Press of Mississippi, 2018)

City of Light Publishing is predicated on the
belief that we can all be a light in the world.

Become a citizen of the City of Light!

Follow @CityofLightPublishing

Go to www.CityofLightPublishing.com
to subscribe to our newsletters.

 The New Idea Press imprint features innovative
nonfiction that explores new ideas, new
perspectives, and new voices.